# 28 DAYS
## *to a*
## CLOSER WALK
## *With God*

**A Devotional to Strengthen Your Faith, Quiet the Noise, and Grow Closer to God**

Copyright © 2025 Triune Publications
All rights reserved.
No part of this publication may be reproduced, stored in a retrieval system, or transmitted in any form or by any means—electronic, mechanical, photocopying, recording, or otherwise—without the prior written permission of the publisher, except in the case of brief quotations used in reviews or articles.
This devotional is intended for personal reflection and spiritual encouragement. It is not intended to replace professional counseling, medical advice, or pastoral care.
Published by Triune Publications
Triune Publications is an imprint of Cosmic Publications, LLC
Printed in the United States of America

**TRIUNE PUBLICATIONS**

Thank you for purchasing out Devotional. As a thank you, please accept this free gift. We do hope it can be a blessing to you.

**SCAN ME**

# CONTENTS

| | |
|---|---|
| Greetings | 5 |
| How to Use This Devotional | 7 |
| Day 1: Draw Near to God | 9 |
| Day 2: God Wants Your Heart, Not Perfection | 13 |
| Day 3: Make Room for God | 17 |
| Day 4: God Is Not Mad at You | 21 |
| Day 5: Speak Honestly with God | 25 |
| Day 6: When You Don't Feel Anything | 29 |
| Day 7: The Closer You Get, the Clearer It Becomes | 33 |
| Day 8: God Is With You in the Waiting | 37 |
| Day 9: God Wants to Speak to You | 41 |
| Day 10: Let God's Word Shape You | 45 |
| Day 11: You're Not Too Broken for God | 49 |
| Day 12: Invite God IntoYour Everyday | 53 |
| Day 13: Obedience Over Outcome | 57 |
| Day 14: Rest Is Spiritual | 61 |
| Day 15: God is Still Writing Your Story | 65 |
| Day 16: You Were Created on Purpose | 69 |
| Day 17: Don't Compare Your Journey | 73 |
| Day 18: God Sees What No One Else Does | 77 |
| Day 19: Worship Is More Than a Song | 81 |
| Day 20: You Are Never Alone | 85 |

| | |
|---|---:|
| Day 21: Let Go of What's Holding You Back | 89 |
| Day 22: Faith Grows in the Struggle | 93 |
| Day 23: Forgiveness Sets You Free | 97 |
| Day 24: God Is Your Provider | 101 |
| Day 25: God Uses Imperfect People | 105 |
| Day 26: Stay Close When It's Quiet | 109 |
| Day 27: Your Life Can Shine | 113 |
| Day 28: This Is Just the Beginning | 117 |
| Conclusion: Keep Walking | 121 |

# Greetings

Hi there,

Thank you for choosing to spend the next 28 days seeking God more intentionally. We're honored to be part of your journey.

This devotional is part of the *28-Day Devotionals for Everyday Faith* series — created to help you pause, reflect, and draw closer to God in the middle of everyday life.

You don't need perfect prayers or long hours of quiet to meet with God. You just need a willing heart. He's already near — and He loves when you take even the smallest step toward Him.

> **"Draw near to God, and He will draw near to you."**
> *— James 4:8*

As you begin, remember this: He sees you. He's for you. And He's walking with you every step of the way.

With grace and gratitude,
Triune Publications

# How to Use This Devotional

Welcome. Whether you're new to faith, returning after a dry season, or simply longing for a deeper connection with God, this devotional is for you. You don't need to be perfect, have all the answers, or set aside hours a day. All you need is a willing heart and a few intentional minutes. God will meet you right where you are.

## The 28-Day Rhythm

Each day of this devotional includes:

- **Scripture Focus** – A verse or passage to ground your heart in truth

- **Devotional Insight** – A short, meaningful reflection to stir your spirit

- **Reflect & Respond** – Journal prompts to help you personalize what you've read

- **Action Step** – A practical, faith-building challenge for the day

- **Prayer for the Day** – A simple, honest prayer to guide your conversation with God

- **Declaration** – A bold truth to speak over your life and carry with you

## How Much Time Will This Take?

Most days will take 10 to 20 minutes. Go at your own pace. If you miss a day, don't feel guilty — simply pick up where you left off. This is not about perfection; it's about presence. God isn't grading your performance. He delights in your pursuit.

## Tips to Get the Most Out of It

- Find a consistent time and quiet space to meet with God each day.

- Be honest. These pages are a safe place. God already knows your heart — this is your chance to share it with Him.

- Write your reflections down. Journaling helps slow you down and allows truth to take root.

- Don't just read about God — talk to Him. Use the prayer and declaration to make it personal.

## One Last Reminder

You're not just doing a devotional — you're showing up for a relationship. Each day you open these pages is an act of drawing near, and God has promised He will draw near to you.

Let's begin.

# Day 1: Draw Near to God

## Scripture Focus

> "Draw near to God, and He will draw near to you."
> — James 4:8

## Devotional Insight

We often assume that God feels distant because He's far away — but what if it's us who have drifted?

Let's be honest, life can distract us: appointments, responsibilities, scrolling screens, emotional exhaustion. Suddenly, you realize you've been running on spiritual fumes, wondering why God seems silent.

But God isn't hiding. He's not punishing you with distance. He's right there — waiting. Waiting for a whisper, a turned heart, a surrendered moment.

The promise in James 4:8 is simple and stunning: if you draw near to God, He will draw near to you. Not might. Not sometimes. He will.

And "drawing near" doesn't have to be complicated. It could be five honest minutes with your Bible. A whispered prayer in traffic. A worship song through tears. A surrender of your agenda. These moments add up — and open up space for intimacy.

Today is not about performance. It's about presence. When you lean in, so does He.

## Reflect & Respond

1. When was the last time you truly felt close to God?

   _____
   _____
   _____
   _____
   _____

2. What distractions or routines tend to keep you from spending time with Him?

   _____
   _____
   _____
   _____
   _____

3. What does "drawing near" look like for you in this season?

   _____
   _____
   _____
   _____
   _____

## Action Step

Create a "God space" in your day — even just 10 minutes. Turn off distractions, open your Bible or journal, and simply sit with Him. Say: "God, I'm here. I want to know You better."

## Prayer for the Day

*Father, I want to know You more. Help me quiet the noise and choose Your presence today. Even if I feel distant, I choose to draw near, trusting that You're drawing near to me. Awaken my heart. In Jesus' name, amen.*

## Declaration

"God wants to be close to me — and today, I'm choosing to be close to Him."

# NOTES

# Day 2: God Wants Your Heart, Not Perfection

## Scripture Focus

"People look at the outward appearance, but the Lord looks at the heart."
— *1 Samuel 16:7*

## Devotional Insight

It's easy to believe the lie that closeness with God depends on our performance — how long we pray, how much we serve, how "good" we've been lately.

But God isn't looking for spiritual perfection. He's looking for sincerity. A humble, open, honest heart.

When Samuel looked at David's older, stronger brothers, he thought surely one of them must be God's chosen. But God reminded him — He sees deeper. He always looks beyond outward appearances and achievements. He sees the heart.

You don't have to fix yourself before coming to God. He's not impressed by spiritual checklists or perfect church attendance. He wants your raw, real, repentant heart — right now.

Today, trade striving for surrender. Give Him the unfiltered version of you. That's the one He's always loved.

## Reflect & Respond

1. Have you ever felt like you needed to "earn" closeness with God?

   _____
   _____
   _____
   _____
   _____

2. What would it look like to approach God just as you are — without trying to fix yourself first?

   _____
   _____
   _____
   _____
   _____

3. What's one part of your heart you've been hiding from Him?

   _____
   _____
   _____
   _____
   _____

## Action Step

Take 5 minutes today to write a raw, honest prayer. No filters. No fancy language. Just you, being real with God. If you're unsure how to start, begin with:
 *"God, here's what's really going on..."*

## Prayer for the Day

God, I often try to clean myself up before I come to You. But You already see it all — and You love me anyway. Help me be honest with You today. I don't want to perform. I want to be close. You can have my heart — every part of it. In Jesus' name, amen.

## Declaration

"God wants the real me, not the perfect me."

# NOTES

# Day 3: Make Room for God

## Scripture Focus

> "Be still, and know that I am God."
> — Psalm 46:10

## Devotional Insight

God often speaks the loudest in the quietest places — but our lives are rarely quiet.

We move from one thing to the next: work, school, appointments, errands, messages, updates, notifications. And somewhere in that whirlwind, our soul gets crowded. It's not that God has stopped speaking… it's that we've stopped listening.

Psalm 46:10 doesn't just suggest stillness; it commands it. Be still. Stop striving. Step back. Slow down.
Because in stillness, we remember who He is — and who we are not.

If you want a closer walk with God, you must create space for Him. Not just a quick nod or a rushed prayer, but real space: in your schedule, in your thoughts, in your home, in your heart.

Stillness isn't wasted time. It's where clarity, conviction, and closeness grow.

## Reflect & Respond

1. What keeps your life so busy or loud that it's hard to hear from God?

   _____
   _____
   _____
   _____

2. When was the last time you were truly still in His presence?

   _____
   _____
   _____
   _____

3. What would it look like for you to "make room" for God today — even in a small way?

   _____
   _____
   _____
   _____
   _____

## Action Step

Set a timer for five minutes and sit in silence with God. No distractions, no requests. Just stillness. Breathe deeply. Let your mind slow down. Focus on the truth: *He is God, and He is near.*

## Prayer for the Day

God, I confess that I've been distracted, busy, and often too loud to hear You. But I want to know You. Teach me to be still. Help me slow down enough to feel Your presence and hear Your voice. I give You space in my day, my mind, and my heart. Amen.

## Declaration

"I will make room for God — because He is worth slowing down for."

# NOTES

# Day 4: God Is Not Mad at You

## Scripture Focus

> "There is now no condemnation for those who are in Christ Jesus."
> — Romans 8:1

## Devotional Insight

Many Christians walk through life with a quiet, heavy question: *Is God disappointed in me?* Maybe you've felt this too.

We mess up. We fall short. We say we'll pray but forget. We struggle with the same sin. And over time, guilt begins to whisper, *"You're not enough. God's tired of you."* If you've ever felt this way, trust me you are not alone.

But that voice isn't from God — it's from shame.

Romans 8:1 is a lifeline of truth. It says there is no condemnation for those who are in Christ. None. Not a little. Not later. Not after you've punished yourself.

If you're in Christ — if you've given your life to Him — then your debt is paid. You are forgiven, loved, and covered in grace.

God doesn't relate to you based on your performance. He relates to you based on Jesus' finished work. And because of that, He isn't angry or withholding. He's welcoming.

There is no need to hide or work harder to be accepted. You already are.

## Reflect & Respond

1. Have you ever felt like God was disappointed in you?

   _____
   _____
   _____
   _____
   _____

2. What's one area where you've been carrying guilt or shame?

   _____
   _____
   _____
   _____
   _____

3. How does today's verse change the way you think about your relationship with God?

   _____
   _____
   _____
   _____
   _____

## Action Step

Write down Romans 8:1 on a notecard or sticky note and place it where you'll see it today. Every time you look at it, say it out loud — as truth over your life.

## Prayer for the Day

Father, thank You that I don't have to live under condemnation. Remind me that Your love isn't based on what I do, but on who You are. Help me to receive Your grace and walk in freedom. I choose to let go of guilt and shame today. Amen.

## Declaration

God is not mad at me — He's madly in love with me.

# NOTES

# Day 5: Speak Honestly with God

## Scripture Focus

"I pour out before him my complaint; before him I tell my trouble."
— Psalm 142:2

## Devotional Insight

Sometimes we think we have to clean up our emotions before bringing them to God — as if He only wants polished prayers with the right tone and timing.

But that's not how David prayed. He poured out his complaints. He told God all his troubles, fears, doubts, and even frustrations. And God wasn't offended — He was present.

Let's be honest — sometimes it feels easier to fake peace than admit we're falling apart. But God invites honesty, not performance. He doesn't want the version of you that wears a mask. He wants the real you — even when you're angry, confused, anxious, or exhausted.

Your relationship with God will grow deeper the moment you stop holding back. He already knows what's in your heart. He's just waiting for you to bring it to Him.

So tell Him everything. Not because He needs the information, but because you need the release.

## Reflect & Respond

1. Do you ever hold back your true feelings when talking to God? Why?

   _____
   _____
   _____
   _____
   _____

2. What's one thing weighing on you right now that you haven't fully brought to Him?

   _____
   _____
   _____
   _____
   _____

3. How would your relationship with God change if you prayed with complete honesty?

   _____
   _____
   _____
   _____
   _____

## Action Step

Set a timer for ten minutes and write a no-filter prayer in your journal or on a blank sheet of paper. Don't worry about sounding "spiritual." Just be honest.

## Prayer for the Day

God, I want to be honest with You — not just polite. You already know everything in my heart, so help me come to You with full honesty and trust. Thank You for listening when I pour it all out. I believe You care, and You are near. Amen.

## Declaration

God can handle my honesty — and He wants my heart, not my filter.

# NOTES

# Day 6: When You Don't Feel Anything

## Scripture Focus

> "Blessed are those who have not seen and yet have believed."
> — John 20:29

## Devotional Insight

There will be days in your walk with God when everything feels dry.

You'll open your Bible and feel nothing. You'll pray and hear silence. You'll worship and wonder if your voice even reaches past the ceiling. These moments are real — and they don't mean something's wrong with you.

Our faith is not built on feelings. It's built on truth.

God never promised you'd always *feel* close to Him. But He did promise He would never leave you. On the days when your emotions are flat, your motivation is low, and your spirit feels dull, your faith still matters. In fact, believing when you don't feel anything is one of the purest forms of faith.

God sees your persistence. He honors your quiet obedience. He treasures your trust even in the silence.

You don't walk by sight. You don't walk by emotion. You walk by faith.

## Reflect & Respond

1. Have you ever felt spiritually "numb" or dry? What was that season like for you?

   _____
   _____
   _____
   _____
   _____

2. How do you usually respond when you feel distant from God?

   _____
   _____
   _____
   _____
   _____

3. What truth can you hold onto when your feelings don't match your faith?

   _____
   _____
   _____
   _____
   _____

## Action Step

Take a moment to thank God — not for what you feel, but for who He is. Write a short list of three truths about God that remain steady even when emotions don't.

## Prayer for the Day

God, even when I don't feel You, I choose to believe You. Help me stay close to You in the dry seasons. Teach me to trust You when it's quiet. Thank You that my feelings don't determine Your faithfulness. I believe You are with me. Amen.

## Declaration

"I will walk by faith — not by feelings."

# NOTES

# Day 7: The Closer You Get, the Clearer It Becomes

## Scripture Focus

> "Your word is a lamp for my feet,
> a light on my path."
> — Psalm 119:105

## Devotional Insight

We often want God to reveal the entire path before we take the first step.
 But God rarely works that way.

He gives light for the next step, not the whole journey. That's why Psalm 119 says His Word is a lamp to our feet — not a floodlight that shows us the entire road ahead.

Let's be real — that can be frustrating. We want clarity, certainty, and a 10-year plan. But it's actually a gift. If God gave us the full picture, we might run ahead of Him, rely on ourselves, or shrink back in fear. Instead, He invites us to walk with Him, one step at a time.

And here's the beautiful part: the closer you walk with Him, the clearer everything else becomes. His peace starts replacing your panic. His truth drowns out the lies. His presence steadies your heart, even when the future feels uncertain.

You don't need to see the whole road — you just need to follow the One holding the lamp.

## *Reflect & Respond*

1. What area of your life feels unclear or uncertain right now?

   _____
   _____
   _____
   _____
   _____

2. How has God given you "just enough light" in past seasons?

   _____
   _____
   _____
   _____
   _____

3. What step of obedience can you take today, even without knowing what comes next?

   _____
   _____
   _____
   _____
   _____

## Action Step

Choose one small area of your life that feels confusing or unsettled. Bring it to God in prayer and ask for just the *next* step. Write down whatever comes to mind and commit to obey it.

## Prayer for the Day

Lord, I want to trust You with what I can't see. Help me stop demanding answers and start following You more closely. Thank You for being my light and guide. Even when the way isn't clear, I know You are. Amen.

## Declaration

I don't need to see the whole path — I just need to stay close to the One lighting it.

# NOTES

# Day 8: God Is With You in the Waiting

## Scripture Focus

"The Lord is good to those who wait for him, to the soul who seeks him."
— Lamentations 3:25

## Devotional Insight

Waiting can feel like wasted time.

You pray, you trust, you hope — but the breakthrough hasn't come. The door stays closed. The answer is delayed. It's tempting to believe God is ignoring you or punishing you.

If you've ever whispered, "God, where are You?" — you're not alone.
But Scripture tells a different story. Lamentations 3:25 reminds us that God is good to those who wait for Him. Not absent. Not cruel. Good.

God isn't just preparing the outcome — He's preparing you. Waiting is often where your roots go deeper, your faith stretches wider, and your character is refined. It's not a punishment. It's preparation.

You might not see it now, but nothing is wasted when it's surrendered to God. He's with you in the waiting. Working. Shaping. Strengthening. And when the time is right, He will open the door no one else can.

## Reflect & Respond

1. What are you currently waiting on God to do or reveal?

   _____
   _____
   _____
   _____
   _____

2. How do you usually respond to waiting — spiritually or emotionally?

   _____
   _____
   _____
   _____
   _____

3. What might God be developing in you *during* the wait?

   _____
   _____
   _____
   _____
   _____

## Action Step

Write a short letter to God expressing what you're waiting for — and then surrender it to Him. End the letter with the phrase: "I trust You, even here."

## Prayer for the Day

Lord, waiting is hard. But I believe You are with me in it. Help me not to waste this season but to lean into You. Strengthen my faith, deepen my patience, and remind me that You are always working — even when I can't see it. Amen.

## Declaration

God is working in the waiting — and I trust Him with the timing.

# NOTES

# Day 9: God Wants to Speak to You

## Scripture Focus

"My sheep listen to my voice; I know them, and they follow me."
— John 10:27

## Devotional Insight

Many Christians wonder, *"Does God really speak to me — or is it just my own thoughts?"*

The truth is: God does speak. He's a relational God, and relationships require communication. He speaks through His Word, through the Holy Spirit, through people, and sometimes even through whispers in your soul.

Jesus said His sheep know His voice. That means it's not reserved for the "super spiritual" or the pastor on stage — it's for you.

The more time you spend with God, the more clearly you'll recognize when He's speaking. Just like you'd recognize the voice of someone you love in a crowded room, you'll begin to notice when it's Him nudging your heart, stirring your spirit, or highlighting a Scripture at just the right time.

Hearing God is not about volume — it's about familiarity. He's speaking. Are you listening?

## Reflect & Respond

1. Have you ever sensed God speaking to you? What did it feel like?

   _____
   _____
   _____
   _____
   _____

2. What helps you slow down and listen to God more intentionally?

   _____
   _____
   _____
   _____
   _____

3. What might God be trying to say to you in this season?

   _____
   _____
   _____
   _____
   _____

## Action Step

Spend five extra minutes in quiet after your prayer time today. Ask God, "What do You want to say to me?" Write down whatever thoughts, scriptures, or impressions come to mind. Don't overanalyze — just listen.

## Prayer for the Day

God, I believe You are still speaking today. Help me to recognize Your voice. Teach me to slow down, listen closely, and trust what You reveal. Thank You that I don't have to guess — You are a God who speaks. Amen.

## Declaration

God is speaking — and I am learning to listen.

# NOTES

# Day 10: Let God's Word Shape You

## Scripture Focus

> "All Scripture is God-breathed and is useful for teaching, rebuking, correcting and training in righteousness."
> — 2 Timothy 3:16

## Devotional Insight

If you want to grow closer to God, you can't skip His Word. It's more than a book. It's breath. It's truth. It's alive.

The Bible isn't just meant to inform you — it's meant to transform you. It teaches you who God is, reveals who you are, and guides you into the life you were created to live. It comforts, convicts, and clarifies.

Let's be honest — it's easy to treat Bible reading like a task to check off. But here's the key: you have to engage it. Not just skim a verse here and there, but open your heart as you open its pages. When you let Scripture read you, not just the other way around, that's when transformation happens.

God's Word reshapes our thinking, realigns our desires, and reminds us what's true when everything around us feels unstable. It becomes our anchor.

So don't treat it like a checklist. Treat it like a conversation — where God speaks, and your heart responds.

## Reflect & Respond

1. How has the Bible impacted your life in the past?

2. What's been your biggest challenge with reading it consistently?

3. What would it look like for you to approach Scripture as a conversation rather than a duty?

## Action Step

Pick a passage that speaks to something you're facing right now (you can start with Psalm 23, Romans 8, or John 15). Read it slowly, then underline or write down one verse that stands out. Spend a few minutes reflecting on why it stood out to you.

## Prayer for the Day

Lord, thank You for giving me Your Word. Help me not to rush past it or treat it as routine. Speak to me through it. Use it to shape my thoughts, my character, and my choices. I want to hear Your voice through every page. Amen.

## Declaration

God's Word is alive — and it's transforming me from the inside out.

# NOTES

# Day 11: You're Not Too Broken for God

## Scripture Focus

"He heals the brokenhearted and binds up their wounds." — Psalm 147:3

## Devotional Insight

There's a lie many believers carry deep down: *"I'm too broken for God to really use or love."*

Maybe you've been hurt, disappointed, or shamed. Maybe your story is messy — full of things you'd rather forget. And maybe somewhere along the way, you began to believe that your pain disqualifies you.

But God sees it all — every wound, every mistake, every scar — and He still draws near. Not to condemn you, but to heal you.

Psalm 147:3 doesn't say He avoids the brokenhearted. It says He binds their wounds. That means God isn't afraid of your mess — He moves toward it.

Jesus didn't come for the perfect. He came for the hurting, the lost, the ashamed, and the weary. He came for you.

Your brokenness doesn't disqualify you — it positions you for His grace. You don't have to hide anymore. You can bring it all to Him.

## Reflect & Respond

1. Have you ever felt "too broken" for God's love or purpose? What led you to that feeling?

   _____
   _____
   _____
   _____
   _____

2. What area of your life still needs healing or restoration?

   _____
   _____
   _____
   _____
   _____

3. What does it look like to let God into that space today?

   _____
   _____
   _____
   _____
   _____

## Action Step

Write down the part of your story you've tried to keep hidden or silent. Then, in prayer, offer it to God — asking Him to begin healing it, redeeming it, and using it for His glory.

## Prayer for the Day

God, sometimes I feel like I've messed up too much or been hurt too deeply to be fully loved. But I believe Your Word. Heal the places in me that still feel broken. Remind me that Your grace is greater than my shame. Thank You for staying close to the hurting — even me. Amen.

## Declaration

My brokenness doesn't disqualify me — it draws God's healing near.

# NOTES

# Day 12: Invite God Into Your Everyday

## Scripture Focus

"Trust in the Lord with all your heart and lean not on your own understanding; in all your ways submit to him, and he will make your paths straight."
— Proverbs 3:5–6

## Devotional Insight

It's easy to treat God like a part of your Sunday routine or your emergency contact in a crisis. But He's not just interested in the spiritual parts of your life — He wants all of it.

Proverbs 3 doesn't say "in some of your ways." It says "in all your ways submit to Him." That means in your parenting, your work, your relationships, your time management, your finances — even your scrolling and your daily decisions.

God wants to walk with you in the ordinary, not just the holy moments. He wants to speak into your schedule, guide your thoughts, and shape your reactions. He doesn't compartmentalize you, so don't compartmentalize Him.

The more you invite God into your day — the mundane and the meaningful — the more your life begins to align with His wisdom, His peace, and His power.

Don't wait for a crisis to call on Him. Invite Him into everything.

## Reflect & Respond

1. Are there areas of your life where you tend to keep God at a distance?

   _____
   _____
   _____
   _____
   _____

2. What would it look like to involve Him more intentionally in your everyday routines?

   _____
   _____
   _____
   _____
   _____

3. What's one daily habit or moment where you can pause and acknowledge God's presence?

   _____
   _____
   _____
   _____
   _____

## Action Step

Pick one simple routine today — like your commute, lunch break, or evening chores — and use it to intentionally talk with God. No agenda. Just include Him.

## Prayer for the Day

Lord, I don't want You to be just a part of my Sunday or my struggles. I want You in my every day. Help me to invite You into the ordinary moments and trust You with every decision. I submit all my ways to You. Walk with me today. Amen.

## Declaration

I will invite God into everything — not just the spiritual parts.

# NOTES

# Day 13: Obedience Over Outcome

## Scripture Focus

"Blessed rather are those who hear the word of God and obey it." — Luke 11:28

## Devotional Insight

We often focus on the outcome: *What will happen if I obey? Will it work out? Will I be blessed? Will others understand?*

But God focuses on the heart: *Will you trust Me enough to obey, even if you don't see the result yet?*

Obedience isn't always glamorous or immediately rewarding. Sometimes it's inconvenient. Sometimes it costs you something — popularity, comfort, or control. But real closeness with God is built through consistent obedience, not just emotional moments.

Luke 11:28 reminds us that blessing follows obedience — not just hearing the Word, but *doing* it.
Even when it's hard.
Even when it doesn't make sense.
Even when you're the only one saying yes.

God's plan is always better than your logic. And obedience, even in the small things, positions you for deeper intimacy with Him.

Don't wait to understand the outcome. Walk in obedience today — and trust God with the rest.

## Reflect & Respond

1. Has there been a time when you obeyed God even though you didn't fully understand? What happened?

   _____
   _____
   _____
   _____
   _____

2. What's something you feel God is asking you to do right now — but you're hesitating?

   _____
   _____
   _____
   _____
   _____

3. What might be holding you back from full obedience?

   _____
   _____
   _____
   _____
   _____

## Action Step

Identify one small act of obedience you've been delaying — and do it today. Make the call. Set the boundary. Forgive. Give. Say yes. Trust God with what comes next.

## Prayer for the Day

God, I want to obey You — not just when it's easy, but when it's hard, uncomfortable, or unclear. Give me courage to say yes to You today. I trust that whatever You ask is for my good and Your glory. Amen.

## Declaration

I choose obedience today — even before I know the outcome.

# NOTES

# Day 14: Rest Is Spiritual

## Scripture Focus

"Come to me, all you who are weary and burdened, and I will give you rest."
— Matthew 11:28

## Devotional Insight

In a culture that idolizes hustle, rest can feel lazy or unproductive.
But to God, rest is sacred.

When Jesus invites the weary to come to Him, He doesn't say, *"I'll give you more strength to push harder."* He says, *"I will give you rest."*

Spiritual maturity isn't proven by burnout. It's nurtured in rhythm. Jesus Himself withdrew often to rest and pray. Not because He was weak — but because He was wise.

God isn't asking you to prove yourself by doing more. He's inviting you to know Him more by slowing down. Your soul needs Sabbath. Your body needs recovery. Your mind needs stillness. And your heart needs space to hear His voice again.

Rest isn't a reward for having everything done — it's a gift you're allowed to receive today.

## Reflect & Respond

1. Do you feel guilty when you rest? Why or why not?

   _____
   _____
   _____
   _____

2. What does rest look like for you — physically, emotionally, and spiritually?

   _____
   _____
   _____
   _____

3. How can you make rest part of your rhythm, not just an occasional emergency break?

   _____
   _____
   _____
   _____

## Action Step

Schedule one intentional rest activity this week: a quiet walk, a tech-free hour, journaling, napping, or simply sitting in God's presence. Protect it like any other appointment — and show up for it.

## Prayer for the Day

God, I've been carrying more than I was meant to. Help me to rest in You today — not just physically, but deep in my soul. Teach me to stop striving and to trust that You are still at work, even when I pause. I receive Your rest. Amen.

## Declaration

Rest is not weakness — it's worship.

# NOTES

# Day 15: God is Still Writing Your Story

## Scripture Focus

"...being confident of this, that he who began a good work in you will carry it on to completion until the day of Christ Jesus."
— Philippians 1:6

## Devotional Insight

It's easy to feel discouraged when life isn't unfolding the way you expected. You look around and wonder if you missed your moment, messed up your calling, or lost too much time.

But here's the truth: God doesn't abandon what He starts.

Philippians 1:6 reminds us that the same God who began a good work in you is still writing — still shaping, still leading, still redeeming. Your current chapter might feel confusing or incomplete, but it's not the end. It's part of the process.

You might not like how this chapter feels — but that doesn't mean it's not part of a beautiful story.
Every story has tension, every journey has setbacks, and every life of faith includes waiting and wondering. But God's hand is on every page.

Even when you can't see how the pieces fit together, He does. And He's not finished.

## Reflect & Respond

1. Where in your life do you feel stuck, unfinished, or behind?

   _____
   _____
   _____
   _____

2. How does it encourage you to know that God is still working — even when it's not visible yet?

   _____
   _____
   _____
   _____

3. What would it look like to trust God with this current chapter of your life?

   _____
   _____
   _____
   _____

## Action Step

Write the phrase "God is still writing my story" somewhere visible — your mirror, phone lock screen, or journal. Every time you see it today, speak it as a reminder of His ongoing work.

## Prayer for the Day

Lord, thank You that You're not done with me. I surrender the unfinished places, the painful pages, and the unanswered questions. Help me trust that You are writing something good — even here. Keep working in me, and give me peace in the process. Amen.

## Declaration

God is not finished — He's still writing my story.

# NOTES

# Day 16: You Were Created on Purpose

## Scripture Focus

> "For we are God's handiwork, created in Christ Jesus to do good works, which God prepared in advance for us to do."
> — Ephesians 2:10

## Devotional Insight

You are not here by accident.
You're not just filling space or surviving life. You were created on purpose — for a purpose.

Ephesians 2:10 says you are God's handiwork. That means you are His masterpiece — intentionally formed, uniquely gifted, and deeply loved. You were created through Christ and *for* Christ — to walk in the good works He planned long before you were born.

That includes your personality, your passions, your story, even your scars. Nothing is wasted when placed in His hands.

When you start to believe this truth, it changes everything. You stop chasing worth through achievement or comparison. You stop shrinking back in fear or shame. You start walking in freedom, with confidence that your life matters — because He says it does.

## Reflect & Respond

1. Have you ever struggled to believe your life has purpose? Why or when?

   _____
   _____
   _____
   _____
   _____

2. What are some unique passions, talents, or experiences God has given you?

   _____
   _____
   _____
   _____
   _____

3. How can you use those today to reflect His love or serve someone else?

   _____
   _____
   _____
   _____
   _____

## Action Step

Make a short list of three "good works" you feel drawn to — big or small — and ask God how you can walk in one of them today. Then take one action toward it.

_____
_____
_____
_____
_____

## Prayer for the Day

Father, thank You for creating me with purpose. Forgive me for the times I've doubted my worth or lived like I was just getting by. Help me believe that I am Your handiwork — and show me how to walk in the good works You've prepared for me. Amen.

## Declaration

I was created on purpose — and I'm here for a reason.

# NOTES

# Day 17: Don't Compare Your Journey

## Scripture Focus

"Let us run with perseverance the race marked out for us, fixing our eyes on Jesus..."
— Hebrews 12:1–2

## Devotional Insight

Nothing will steal your joy and stunt your growth faster than comparison.

It sneaks in quietly. You see someone else's marriage, ministry, success, or spiritual life and start to wonder, *Why not me? Why am I behind? What am I missing?*

But God didn't call you to run their race. He called you to run yours.

Hebrews 12 says to run the race marked out for us — not for someone else. Your path will look different. Your pace may be slower or faster. Your challenges and callings will be uniquely designed for your growth, not for your competition.

And let's face it — comparison is exhausting. It keeps you striving instead of trusting.
The key isn't to look left or right — it's to fix your eyes on Jesus. Because when you focus on Him, you stop obsessing over how far everyone else is ahead (or behind).

Freedom comes when you stop comparing and start obeying — right where you are.

## Reflect & Respond

1. In what area of life are you most tempted to compare yourself to others?

___

2. How has comparison affected your confidence or spiritual walk?

___

3. What would it look like to fully embrace the path God has given *you*?

___

## Action Step

Every time you catch yourself comparing today, pause and pray:

"God, thank You for my race. Help me run it with perseverance and joy."

Write this prayer somewhere visible as a reminder.

## Prayer for the Day

God, I confess that I often compare myself to others. I lose sight of what You've called me to do and who You've created me to be. Help me fix my eyes on You — not on people. Give me strength to run my race with perseverance and purpose. Amen.

## Declaration

I was never meant to compete — I was created to complete the race God gave me.

# NOTES

# Day 18: God Sees What No One Else Does

## Scripture Focus

"The eyes of the Lord are on the righteous, and his ears are attentive to their cry."
— Psalm 34:15

## Devotional Insight

Sometimes it feels like no one notices.
The late-night prayers. The quiet faithfulness. The effort to do the right thing when it would be easier not to.

But just because it's not being applauded doesn't mean it's not being seen.
**God sees. Every single moment.**

Psalm 34:15 reminds us that His eyes are on the righteous — not just the famous, not just the loud, but the faithful. His ears are attentive to your cry, even the ones that never leave your lips.

You may feel overlooked by people, but you are *seen* by God.
 You may feel like your effort isn't making a difference, but God honors obedience, even when it's invisible to everyone else.

Keep showing up. Keep being faithful. Keep choosing integrity.
He sees you. And His approval matters more than anyone else's applause.

## Reflect & Respond

1. Where in your life do you feel unseen or unappreciated?

   _____
   _____
   _____
   _____
   _____

2. How does it encourage you to know God notices every act of faithfulness?

   _____
   _____
   _____
   _____
   _____

3. What would change if you truly believed His attention was always on you?

   _____
   _____
   _____
   _____
   _____

## Action Step

Write a short note to yourself (or speak it aloud): "God sees me when I _____." Fill in the blank with something no one else may notice — but you do faithfully. Post it where you'll be reminded.

## Prayer for the Day

God, thank You for seeing what no one else does. When I feel invisible, remind me that You are watching with love and delight. Help me live for Your eyes, not the world's approval. I trust that nothing I do for You is ever wasted. Amen.

## Declaration

Even when no one else sees me — God does, and that's enough.

# NOTES

# Day 19: Worship Is More Than a Song

## Scripture Focus

"Therefore, I urge you, brothers and sisters, in view of God's mercy, to offer your bodies as a living sacrifice, holy and pleasing to God—this is your true and proper worship."
— Romans 12:1

## Devotional Insight

When we think of worship, we often think of singing.
 Hands raised, music playing, emotions stirred. And yes, that's part of it — but it's **not all of it**.

True worship goes beyond the music. It's not just a song you sing; it's a life you offer.

Romans 12:1 reminds us that real worship is about offering ourselves — our choices, our actions, our obedience — as a living sacrifice. That means the way you treat people, the way you steward your time, your thoughts, your responses, your priorities... all of it can be an act of worship.

You don't have to be on a stage or in a sanctuary to worship. You can worship in the way you forgive. In how you serve your family. In the attitude you bring to your work. In the way you say "yes" to God when no one else is watching.

Worship isn't just what happens on Sunday. It's how you live on Monday.

## Reflect & Respond

1. What's your current view of worship — and how has it been shaped?

   _____
   _____
   _____
   _____
   _____

2. What areas of your daily life could be transformed into worship if you surrendered them to God?

   _____
   _____
   _____
   _____
   _____

3. How can you intentionally worship God outside of music this week?

   _____
   _____
   _____
   _____
   _____

## Action Step

Pick one ordinary task today — like cleaning, driving, or working — and turn it into worship by inviting God into it. Do it with excellence, gratitude, and awareness of His presence.

## Prayer for the Day

God, I want my life to be worship — not just my words. Help me surrender every part of my day to You. Show me how to honor You in the way I live, speak, serve, and love. Let my actions reflect Your mercy and goodness. Amen.

## Declaration

Worship isn't just a song I sing — it's the life I live.

# NOTES

# Day 20: You Are Never Alone

## Scripture Focus

> "Never will I leave you; never will I forsake you."
> — Hebrews 13:5

## Devotional Insight

Loneliness doesn't always come from being physically alone. You can be surrounded by people and still feel invisible. Still feel misunderstood. Still feel like no one really gets you.

But even in your most isolated moments, you are not truly alone.
God's promise in Hebrews 13:5 isn't vague or conditional — it's clear and unwavering: *Never will I leave you. Never will I forsake you.*

That means when the text doesn't come... He's there.
When the room is silent... He's near. When you feel like no one notices or cares... He does.

Don't confuse silence with abandonment — God is often closest when you feel it the least. His presence isn't just a theological idea. It's a daily reality — whether or not you feel it. He is beside you in the ordinary, ahead of you in the unknown, and within you through His Spirit.

You may feel forgotten, but you are held. You may feel overlooked, but you are loved.

## Reflect & Respond

1. When have you felt most alone — and how did you respond?

   _____
   _____
   _____
   _____
   _____

2. How does God's promise to never leave you speak to your current season?

   _____
   _____
   _____
   _____
   _____

3. What's one way you can remind yourself of His presence today?

   _____
   _____
   _____
   _____
   _____

## Action Step

Write a short note from God's perspective to yourself. Start with: *"I am with you, even when..."* and finish the sentence. Keep it where you'll see it often.

_____

_____

_____

_____

_____

## Prayer for the Day

Father, thank You for staying close when I feel far from everything else. Remind me that You are near — even when I can't feel You. Help me walk through today with confidence that I am never alone. Amen.

## Declaration

I am never alone — God is always with me.

# NOTES

# Day 21: Let Go of What's Holding You Back

## Scripture Focus

"Let us throw off everything that hinders and the sin that so easily entangles. And let us run with perseverance the race marked out for us."
— Hebrews 12:1

## Devotional Insight

Sometimes the things slowing us down spiritually aren't always obvious sins. Sometimes they're distractions. Sometimes they're people-pleasing, fear, comfort zones, or old stories we keep telling ourselves.

Hebrews 12 challenges us to throw off what's hindering us — not to manage it or make peace with it, but to release it. Why? Because you were made to run — not carry what was never meant for you.

Take a moment and really think about that — what are you dragging that God never asked you to carry?
There is a race marked out for you. A purpose. A calling. A closeness with God that's waiting on the other side of obedience. But you can't run freely while clinging to what holds you back.

Letting go isn't always easy — but it's worth it. The lighter your heart, the more focused your path. The more you release, the more room God has to move in your life.

## Reflect & Respond

1. What's one thing (habit, fear, relationship, mindset) that's been holding you back in your walk with God?

   _____
   _____
   _____
   _____

2. Why is it hard to let go of that thing? What do you fear losing?

   _____
   _____
   _____
   _____

3. What freedom might be waiting on the other side of surrender?

   _____
   _____
   _____
   _____

## Action Step

Name one specific thing God may be asking you to release. Write it down. Then pray over it and take one small step today to begin letting go — even if it's just a conversation, boundary, or pause.

## Prayer for the Day

God, I don't want to carry anything that's keeping me from You. Show me what's weighing me down, and give me the courage to release it. Help me run freely in the direction of Your purpose, without fear or hesitation. Amen.

## Declaration

I will let go of what's holding me back — and run the race God has marked out for me.

# NOTES

# Day 22: Faith Grows in the Struggle

## Scripture Focus

> "Consider it pure joy, my brothers and sisters, whenever you face trials of many kinds, because you know that the testing of your faith produces perseverance."
> — James 1:2–3

## Devotional Insight

No one asks for trials. No one signs up for struggle.
But the truth is, some of the deepest growth in your walk with God will happen *because* of the hard seasons — not in spite of them.

James doesn't tell us to enjoy pain, but to find joy in what it produces. Trials refine you. They strip away what's shallow. They teach you to depend, to pray, to trust — not just when it's easy, but when it costs something.

Every test of faith is also a chance for growth.
Not because God is cruel, but because He is committed to shaping you into the person He designed you to be.

If you're struggling right now, don't assume God is distant. He's closer than ever — working in the deep places of your soul, strengthening your roots, and preparing you for what's ahead.

## Reflect & Respond

1. What trial or struggle are you currently facing — or have recently come through?

   _____
   _____
   _____
   _____

2. How has God used struggle in the past to grow your faith?

   _____
   _____
   _____
   _____

3. What fruit (like perseverance, patience, humility) might He be producing in you now?

   _____
   _____
   _____
   _____

## Action Step

Take 5 minutes to write down three things your current or past struggle has taught you. Turn those lessons into a short prayer of gratitude — even if it's still hard.

## Prayer for the Day

God, I don't always understand why things are hard, but I choose to trust that You are using this for my good. Grow my faith through the struggle. Shape me through the challenge. And give me eyes to see how You're at work in it all. Amen.

## Declaration

My struggle is not the end of the story — it's the soil where my faith grows.

# NOTES

# Day 23: Forgiveness Sets You Free

## Scripture Focus

"Be kind and compassionate to one another, forgiving each other, just as in Christ God forgave you." — Ephesians 4:32

## Devotional Insight

Forgiveness isn't saying what happened was okay. It's saying you're no longer going to carry it.

Holding on to unforgiveness doesn't punish the other person — it keeps you in chains. It clogs your heart, poisons your peace, and blocks your closeness with God.

Ephesians 4:32 reminds us why we forgive: because we've been forgiven. Not because they apologized. Not because they deserve it. Not because it's easy. But because Jesus showed us mercy we didn't earn.

You might not feel ready — and that's okay. Forgiveness often begins with willingness, not emotion. Forgiveness doesn't mean trust is instantly restored. It doesn't erase the pain. But it does release the power that offense has over you.

It's not a one-time decision. It's a process. And sometimes, it's something you choose again and again — not for their sake, but for your own healing.

## Reflect & Respond

1. Is there someone you've been holding resentment toward — even quietly?

   _____
   _____
   _____
   _____
   _____

2. What has unforgiveness cost you emotionally, spiritually, or relationally?

   _____
   _____
   _____
   _____
   _____

3. What would change in your heart if you started the process of forgiving?

   _____
   _____
   _____
   _____
   _____

## Action Step

Write the name (or initials) of someone you need to forgive. Then, speak this aloud in prayer:
"God, I choose to forgive ____. Help me release the hurt and move forward in freedom."

You may need to pray this daily. That's okay.

## Prayer for the Day

God, You forgave me when I didn't deserve it — and now You're calling me to do the same. I don't want to carry bitterness or let past wounds control me. Give me the strength to forgive, to heal, and to walk in freedom. Amen.

## Declaration

Forgiveness doesn't make them right — it makes me free.

# NOTES

# Day 24: God Is Your Provider

## Scripture Focus

"And my God will meet all your needs according to the riches of his glory in Christ Jesus." — Philippians 4:19 (NIV)

## Devotional Insight

Provision isn't just about money — it's about trust.

When life feels uncertain, bills stack up, or the future feels foggy, it's easy to fall into fear. But Philippians 4:19 is a powerful reminder that God doesn't leave His people lacking. He doesn't promise to meet your wants — He promises to meet your needs.

And not barely — but according to *His riches*, not your resources.

This doesn't mean life will always be easy or your bank account will always be full. But it does mean you can rest instead of striving. Because the same God who fed the 5,000, who rained manna from heaven, who provided water from a rock — is still providing today.

Sometimes He meets needs miraculously. Other times through hard work, community, or unexpected doors. But it all flows from Him.

Provision starts with trust. Trust leads to peace. And peace keeps you walking in faith — even before you see the supply.

## Reflect & Respond

1. What need in your life are you currently trusting God to provide for?

   _____
   _____
   _____
   _____

2. What tends to worry you most when it comes to provision or resources?

   _____
   _____
   _____
   _____

3. How have you seen God provide for you in the past — big or small?

   _____
   _____
   _____
   _____

## Action Step

Write out Philippians 4:19 and place it somewhere you'll see often. Let it remind you to speak *faith* over your needs, not fear. Today, practice gratitude for what God has already provided.

## Prayer for the Day

God, You are my source. Not my job, not my bank account, not my own efforts — You. I trust You to meet my needs, even when I can't see how. Teach me to rely on You more and fear less. Thank You for being my faithful Provider. Amen.

## Declaration

I trust God to provide — because He always takes care of His own.

# NOTES

# Day 25: God Uses Imperfect People

## Scripture Focus

"But he said to me, 'My grace is sufficient for you, for my power is made perfect in weakness."— 2 Corinthians 12:9

## Devotional Insight

If you're waiting to feel "good enough" before God can use you — you'll be waiting forever.

Throughout the Bible, God used ordinary, broken, unqualified people to accomplish extraordinary things. Moses stuttered. David messed up big. Peter was impulsive. Paul had a past. Yet God chose them — not because of their strength, but in spite of their weakness.

Why? Because when God works through imperfect people, He gets the glory.

2 Corinthians 12:9 reminds us that God's power shows up best when we admit our weakness. That's when we stop pretending. That's when grace gets real. That's when others see the difference God makes.

You don't have to have it all together. You don't need a platform or a perfect past. You just need to say yes — and trust that His grace will carry you.

## Reflect & Respond

1. What weakness or flaw have you believed disqualifies you from being used by God?

_____
_____
_____
_____

2. How have you seen God work through your imperfections in the past?

_____
_____
_____
_____

3. What would change if you stopped hiding your weakness and let God use it?

_____
_____
_____
_____

## Action Step

Write a short prayer of surrender that starts with:
"God, I give You my weakness — especially _____."
Be honest. Then invite Him to use it for His glory.

_____

_____

_____

_____

_____

## Prayer for the Day

God, I often feel too flawed or unqualified to be used by You. But I believe what Your Word says — that Your grace is enough and Your strength shows up in my weakness. Use every imperfect part of me to reflect Your perfect love. Amen.

## Declaration

God doesn't need me to be perfect — just willing.

# NOTES

# Day 26: Stay Close When It's Quiet

## Scripture Focus

"The Lord is good to those whose hope is in him, to the one who seeks him; it is good to wait quietly for the salvation of the Lord."
— Lamentations 3:25–26

## Devotional Insight

There are seasons when God feels silent.
You pray — no answer.
You seek — no breakthrough.
You wait — and still, nothing changes.

But silence doesn't mean absence. And waiting doesn't mean you've been forgotten.

Lamentations reminds us that it is good to wait quietly. Why? Because something happens in the quiet that doesn't happen in the noise. Your faith deepens. Your roots grow. Your ears become more tuned to His whisper.

If you're in one of those quiet seasons now, don't assume God is far — it may be that He's closer than ever, just working in ways you can't see yet.

God often does His most powerful work below the surface. He's preparing you. Positioning you. Strengthening your trust. You may not feel it, but He's still moving.

So don't walk away when it's quiet. Lean in closer. He hasn't left you — He's leading you.

## Reflect & Respond

1. Have you ever gone through a spiritually "quiet" season? What was it like?

   _____
   _____
   _____
   _____
   _____

2. How do you typically respond when you don't feel or hear God?

   _____
   _____
   _____
   _____
   _____

3. What could God be teaching or developing in you during a season of silence?

   _____
   _____
   _____
   _____

## Action Step

Find a quiet moment today — even just five minutes. Sit in stillness, breathe deeply, and simply say, "God, I'm still here. And I know You are too."
 No requests. Just presence.

## Prayer for the Day

God, help me trust You even when I don't hear You. When everything feels quiet, remind me that You are still near. Strengthen my heart to wait well, and deepen my faith in the silence. I know You are working, even when I can't see it. Amen.

## Declaration

Even in the silence, God is still with me — and I will stay close.

# NOTES

# Day 27: Your Life Can Shine

## Scripture Focus

"In the same way, let your light shine before others, that they may see your good deeds and glorify your Father in heaven."
— Matthew 5:16

## Devotional Insight

You don't have to be loud to make an impact.
You don't need a stage, a platform, or a spotlight to shine for God.

Jesus said your light shines through how you live — the way you speak, serve, love, and show up with integrity. It's the quiet encouragement, the unnoticed act of kindness, the forgiveness no one else sees, the decision to do what's right when it would be easier not to.

**It might not feel like much, but your faithfulness in the small things speaks louder than you realize.**

In a dark world, even a small light stands out. And when you live in a way that reflects God's heart, people won't just notice you — they'll be drawn to Him.

You don't shine to impress others. You shine to point them to the One who lit your life with grace and truth.

You don't have to be perfect. You just have to be willing. And when you walk closely with God, your life becomes a light without you even trying.

## Reflect & Respond

1. What are some "everyday" ways your life reflects God to others?

   _____
   _____
   _____
   _____

2. Where do you feel God calling you to be a light right now — in your family, work, community, or online?

   _____
   _____
   _____
   _____

3. What might be dimming your light, and how can you surrender that to God?

   _____
   _____
   _____
   _____

## Action Step

Do one intentional act of kindness today — anonymously, if possible. Let it be a reminder that your light matters, and God can use even small things to reveal His love.

## Prayer for the Day

God, help my life reflect Your light. Let my words, choices, and actions draw people closer to You. Show me how to live with purpose, love with boldness, and shine with humility. Use me today to point someone to You. Amen.

## Declaration

I don't shine for attention — I shine to reflect God.

# NOTES

# Day 28: This Is Just the Beginning

## Scripture Focus

> "Being rooted and established in love... you may have power... to grasp how wide and long and high and deep is the love of Christ."
> — Ephesians 3:17–18

## Devotional Insight

You made it. Twenty-eight days of showing up, seeking God, and growing deeper. But this isn't the finish line — it's the foundation.

A closer walk with God isn't a one-time decision or a completed devotional. It's a daily relationship. A journey of becoming more rooted in His love, more confident in His presence, and more open to His leading.

Ephesians 3 reminds us that God's love is *limitless*. You can't outgrow it. You can't exhaust it. And there will always be more of Him to discover — more peace, more wisdom, more strength, more joy, more purpose.

So don't stop here. Keep going.
Keep showing up.
Keep listening.
Keep trusting.
Let today be a declaration that you've only just begun.

## Reflect & Respond

1. What has God revealed to you during these 28 days?

   _____
   _____
   _____
   _____
   _____

2. How has your perspective, your heart, or your faith shifted?

   _____
   _____
   _____
   _____
   _____

3. What commitment can you make to continue walking closely with God from here?

   _____
   _____
   _____
   _____
   _____

## Action Step

Write a short "commitment statement" to God. Something simple like:
"Lord, I want to keep walking with You daily. Help me stay close, stay hungry, and stay faithful — one step at a time."

Post it somewhere visible as a reminder of what you've started.

## Prayer for the Day

Father, thank You for walking with me over these 28 days. Thank You for every moment of growth, conviction, healing, and grace. Help me keep seeking You beyond these pages. Let my relationship with You go deeper and my life reflect Your love in everything I do. Amen.

## Declaration

This is not the end — it's just the beginning of a closer walk with God.

# NOTES

# Conclusion: Keep Walking

You made it — 28 days of showing up, reflecting, listening, and leaning in.

But let's be clear: this isn't the end.
This is where your journey with God deepens, widens, and becomes even more real.

Over the past four weeks, you've learned how to hear His voice in the quiet, trust Him in the waiting, forgive what's hard to release, and walk with Him one faithful step at a time. You've learned that closeness with God isn't about being perfect — it's about being present.

And if you're thinking, "I didn't do every day perfectly" — that's okay. Really. This was never about checking boxes. It was about creating space. And if you showed up at all — even tired, messy, or unsure — God met you there.

The same God who walked with you through these pages will walk with you into your next season. He's not just the God of your devotional time — He's the God of your kitchen, your commute, your phone calls, your late nights, and your early mornings.

He's not going anywhere.

## So What's Next?

Here are three simple ways to keep walking closely with God:

- Stay rooted in the Word. Don't let your Bible get dusty. Even five minutes with Scripture can anchor your soul more than an hour on social media.

- Talk to God like He's right there — because He is.
  You don't need perfect prayers. Just honest ones. Keep the conversation going throughout your day.

- Keep your heart soft. Stay open to conviction, correction, and encouragement. God will speak — through His Word, through others, and through your own spirit.

## Final Thoughts

You don't have to rush to the next big thing. Let this season settle into your spirit. Let what God started in you continue to grow — slowly, deeply, steadily.

Because closeness with God isn't built overnight. It's built in the quiet moments when you choose Him again and again.

Even when life gets busy.
Even when you feel nothing.
Even when it's hard to believe.

Keep showing up. He always will.

## A Final Prayer

God, thank You for walking with me through these 28 days. I want more of You — not just in devotionals, but in every part of my life. Help me stay close. Keep me grounded in Your Word, sensitive to Your voice, and bold in my obedience. Draw me deeper still. In Jesus' name, amen.

## A Final Declaration

This is not the end. It's a beginning. And I choose to walk closely with God — one step at a time.

## We'd Love Your Feedback

If *28 Days to a Closer Walk with God* encouraged your heart, helped you grow in your faith, or gave you a fresh perspective in your walk with God — would you take a minute to leave a quick review?

Your voice matters.
Every review helps other readers discover this devotional and gives them the confidence to begin their own journey toward deeper connection with God.

Here's how to share your feedback:

- Go to the Amazon product page

- Scroll to the reviews section

- Click "Write a review" and share a few honest thoughts about your experience

It doesn't need to be long — just real.
Even one or two sentences can help someone decide to take the next step with God.

## Ready for What's Next?

If you're hungry to keep growing, don't stop here.

We created a follow-up devotional just for you:

# *28 Days to Unshakable Peace*

*A journey to quiet the noise, calm your anxious thoughts, and find steady confidence in God's presence — no matter what life throws at you.*

You can start it right away — or whenever your heart needs a reset. Find it now by searching the title on Amazon.

Thank you for walking through these 28 days with us. We're praying that your journey with God continues — with deeper peace, stronger faith, and more daily encounters with His love.

With gratitude,
Triune Publications

www.ingramcontent.com/pod-product-compliance
Lightning Source LLC
Chambersburg PA
CBHW050342010526
44119CB00049B/665